your move

4 questions to ask when you don't know what to do

PARTICIPANT'S GUIDE

Andy Stanley

ZONDERVAN.com/
AUTHORTRACKER
follow your favorite authors

ZONDERVAN

Your Move Participant's Guide
Copyright © 2010 by North Point Ministries, Inc.

Requests for information should be addressed to:
Zondervan, *Grand Rapids, Michigan 49530*

ISBN 978-0-310-40849-9

Cover and interior design by Brian Manley (funwithrobots.com)

Printed in the United States of America

10 11 12 13 14 15 /QG/ 23 22 21 20 19 18 17 16 15 14 13 12 11 10 9 8 7 6 5 4 3 2 1

CONTENTS

INTRODUCTION

Forced to Decide
by Andy Stanley

Life's all about making decisions, isn't it?

If you listen closely to people telling their life stories, you become aware that they're just a sequence of decisions. They reach forks in the road, they make choices that turn out to be defining moments for them, and then they move on—only to encounter the next fork in the road, the next choice, and the next defining moment.

Over and over it happens.

Looking Back Later

Sometimes it's only much later that we realize how big these decisions really were in our lives.

We can look back and be glad about a certain choice we made, because of all the good things it led to—things we could not anticipate in the rush of the moment. Now we wonder, *What if I'd said no to that opportunity back then instead of yes?* Our hearts might even

skip a beat when we realize what we almost did or where a different

choice might have taken us.

There might also be a past choice that we wish we could go back

and change, because it set our lives on a trajectory we never wanted

them to take. We'd give anything to go back and rethink that job of-

fer, that investment opportunity, or that relationship we plunged into.

The truth is, these choices have huge ramifications. They can

lead us along the path to greatness, or they can lead us to ruin and

insignificance. They can direct us toward something we'll end up be-

ing really proud of, or plunge us into something we'll be ashamed to

later admit.

Catching Us Off Guard

These decisions can be so significant and so much can hang in the

balance—yet so often they're triggered by situations that were never

on our radar screens. They come on us by surprise, and we're caught

off guard, yet we have to decide one way or another. They're deci-

sions we didn't plan for and never wanted to make, but ultimately

can't avoid. And, over time, after the dust finally settles and we finally

catch our breath, we find our lives going in completely new direc-

tions.

When these kinds of decisions are forced on us, the schedule always seems too compressed for them. Our time is limited; our options are limited; our information's limited. We wish we could know more—especially about the future.

But we can't. And the pressure's intense: *You have to decide, and decide now.*

It's your move.

Unwelcome Realities

We find our lives punctuated all too often by the kinds of realities that bring these dilemmas.

Maybe your financial condition suddenly tanked and you're forced to make some unexpected lifestyle adjustments.

You're in a relationship and falling in love, but one day you find your parents or your best friend telling you they really don't think this person's right for you. Suddenly you find yourself in a tug-of-war: Do I follow my heart, or follow the advice of some folks who've always cared for me?

Or you could find yourself with someone who's pushing you to go further and faster in a relationship than you're comfortable with. You feel so much tension; you don't want to lose him or her, but at the same time you're not ready to move forward that far and that fast.

Maybe you have a secure job that's a perfect fit for you, but then a friend calls from another city to say he's starting a company. He wants you to join him in a position that he needs to fill right away. It's risky, it's questionable, and it would require you to move, but it's also potentially lucrative. Now you have a choice to make.

Or you're in college, and your parents have been helping out financially to keep you there, but now their finances aren't going so well. What do you do?

Getting Better Prepared

Is there any way to prepare for these surprise situations and the decisions they force—decisions that suddenly become the defining moments of our lives?

I believe there is a way to prepare. In the weeks ahead, I'm going to give you four important questions to remember and return to in those critical moments. They're actually useful and appropriate to ask in regard to any decision you're making, but they're especially designed to help when you're faced with those decisions you don't really want to make, the kind you never thought you'd have to make— when you're short on time and short on information, yet so much is at stake.

All four of these questions are supported in the Bible. As we look together at the biblical evidence, I hope you'll discover in a fresh way just how full the Bible is of insight and wisdom for all of life—including those scary, big-decision moments.

SESSION 1

Really

We're looking together at four questions that are especially helpful to ask when we face decisions that confront us by surprise and that we don't like having to make.

The first of these questions is this: *Am I being completely honest with myself?*

This question is foundational to all the others, yet it's also the most difficult—because it exposes our lack of "self-honesty." The fact is, we spend tremendous amounts of time and energy deceiving ourselves. The reality is, we talk ourselves into a countless number of bad decisions.

Just think of the unnecessary and unwise purchases you've made by convincing yourself in those moments what good deals they were. Or that piece of cake you justified by telling yourself you didn't want to hurt your hostess's feelings. Or the after-work trip to the gym you skipped simply by thinking how nice it would be to get home earlier.

In moments like these, we seldom admit the real reason we're doing it: "I'm lazy and I lack self-control." Instead, we make up whatever reasons we need to justify doing what we really want to do—and then we swallow those silly reasons whole. Right?

Let's do ourselves a favor by finding out how to change those deception dynamics.

DISCUSSION STARTER

When you're tempted to make a choice that's not wise for your physical health or your financial well-being, what kind of justifications will typically enter your mind?

VIDEO OVERVIEW

For Session 1 of the DVD

Here's the first of the four questions:

Am I being completely honest with myself?

We're all experts at selling ourselves on whatever we really want to do, whether we *should* do it or not. We're all very good at deceiving ourselves, because we feel so compelled to justify our unwise decisions. It's as if our hearts are wrapped around a certain choice, then they send our brains a message that says, "Quick, find me some reasons for it!" Our brains manufacture the reasons, and then we start believing them.

Why aren't we more honest with ourselves? Because for the most part, we're on a quest not for truth, but for happiness. Our hearts cling to whatever choices we think will make us happiest, no matter how unwise they might be.

So, we need to ask ourselves, *Why am I doing this . . . really?* What's the *real* reason for the choice I'm making?

We don't often ask ourselves this because it's convicting and uncomfortable. There are times we don't really *want* to know why we're making a certain choice.

There's a deeper reason this question is difficult for us: *There's something wrong with us.*

We're reminded of this inherent weakness in a passage from the book of Jeremiah, a prophet who lived during a time when God was judging the nation of Israel. The people had abandoned worship of the one true God, and through Jeremiah, God reminded them that the main issue in life is always, *Who will you worship?*

Against that backdrop, God makes this statement through his prophet: "The heart is deceitful above all things and beyond cure. Who can understand it?" (Jeremiah 17:9).

Each of us is born with an incurably deceitful heart. We'll never escape that affliction by becoming more mature, more educated, more spiritual, more religious, or more wealthy. With every decision we make, we have the capacity for self-deceit.

But if we'll learn to ask ourselves, *Why* am I doing this? Am I being *completely honest* with myself? we'll find that line of questioning to be liberating . . . as well as terrifying.

It's liberating because any lie we carry always grows more powerful over time; by exposing it, we loosen its dark hold over us.

And it's terrifying because we make ourselves accountable to truth. Jesus said, "You will know the truth, and the truth will set you free" (John 8:32). There's just something healthy and liberating about finally being honest.

So, you need to have a heart-to-heart talk with yourself—aloud, while you're alone and in front of a mirror. Stop ignoring the real reasons behind what you've been doing. Stop lying to yourself. Admit the truth. And when you finally do, those old lies will start losing their power, and you'll go on to make better decisions.

VIDEO NOTES

JEREMIAH - A PROFET
600 BC - JUDAH
WHEN GOD WAS JUDGING ISRAEL
605 BC
605 BC. NEBIKEYMELER RULED
JEREMIAH TRIED TO LET ISAEL
BACK TO GOD

IT FACT IS PERMANENTLY BROKEN
NOT DISHONEST, BUT BROKEN

DISCUSSION QUESTIONS

1. If you're willing to share this with the group, what are some of the most unexpected and uncomfortable decisions you've had to make? In contrast, of all your life's most significant decisions, which were the *easiest* to make?

   WORK, JOB CHANGE

2. What choices in your life are you most grateful for? And how close did you come to making an entirely different decision?

3. In your observation, what are some of the reasons people often seem reluctant to be fully honest with themselves about the reasons for the choices they make?

4. When it's time to make a major decision, what helps you to be more honest with yourself as you consider your true motives and desires?

5. Do you know people who seem more committed to seeking truth than they are to seeking their own happiness?

6. What most convinces you that the human heart is inclined toward self-deception?

MILEPOSTS

- We'll always have the propensity and capacity to lie to ourselves. But we can conquer that by consciously choosing to tell ourselves the truth.

- As we feel inclined toward a particular choice or direction, it's wise to ask, "Why am I doing this . . . really?"

- Being honest with ourselves opens us up to greater freedom and a greater experience of God's grace.

MOVING FORWARD

You might be facing some tough and significant choices right now in your life, or you see them approaching very soon on the horizon. How will it affect your decision-making process to ask the question: "Am I being completely honest with myself?"

And if you're *not* currently facing such a choice, how can you be better prepared to ask this question when you *do* suddenly encounter tough and unexpected decisions that must be made?

CHANGING YOUR MIND

This session's key Scripture passage reminds us of our urgent need for honest self-evaluation:

The heart is deceitful above all things
and beyond cure. Who can understand it?
Jeremiah 17:9

PREPARATION FOR SESSION 2

To help you get ready for Session 2, use these suggested devotions during the week leading up to your small group meeting.

Day One

Read Genesis 37 for the beginning of the dramatic life story of Joseph. What significant and defining qualities do you see in Joseph, in his brothers, and in his father?

Day Two

Joseph's story resumes in Genesis 39. Read the first six verses of this chapter. What evidence do you see of God's involvement in Joseph's life? Do you think we can count on the same degree of involvement from God in our lives today?

Day Three

Joseph's core character is especially on display in Genesis 39:6–10. In your own words, how would you describe the governing motives and principles in his life?

Day Four

In Genesis 39:11–23, Joseph's life reaches another climax and moves swiftly into the consequences. Again, what evidence do you see of God's involvement in Joseph's life, and how does that compare with what we can expect from God?

Day Five

The remaining chapters in Genesis (40–50) continue Joseph's amazing story. Glance over these chapters to see how God rewarded Joseph and how he dealt with Joseph's brothers and his father. How would you say God is most honored by Joseph's life story?

Last Session

In a significant decision-making time, if we'll ask ourselves, *Am I being completely honest with myself?* we'll find more freedom and more of God's grace.

SESSION 2

The Story of Your Life

Every season of life we go through is filled with experiences that at the time are packed with meaning and significance. But later, if we were asked to summarize those experiences, we'd probably condense everything that happened to just a few sentences. Isn't that amazing?

It could be your entire high school experience, your college years, how you got to know the person you ended up marrying, or how you launched into a particular career—whatever it is, huge chunks of our lives get compressed into only a couple of lines. Imagine five years of your life shared in five minutes of conversation!

And what will that conversation sound like? Will you feel the urge to hide some of the truth, because of choices you've made and now regret? Or will you be able to talk about decisions and choices that are honoring to God?

Your current season of life might be one that's full of heartache, trouble, and lingering pain. You struggle to know how to respond to some hard choices that are bearing down on you. But remember: eventually you'll move past all this, and at some point down the road, this tough time will simply be another part of your story. What will you be saying about it?

Let's see what we can learn together about writing our stories well.

DISCUSSION STARTER

When you hear people tell their life stories, what aspects do you generally enjoy hearing about most, and why?

VIDEO OVERVIEW

For Session 2 of the DVD

When we face those tough, unwanted decisions, the second question we need to ask is this:

What story do I want to tell?

As we said before, when people tell their life stories, they condense large chunks of their lives into just a few sentences. Decisions that at the moment seem so large and complicated will later be nothing more than a line or two in the stories we tell. What do we want those stories to say?

In every transition and every decision-making environment, we're writing the script for that story.

Our stories have already developed in a certain way up to this point. But often, as we face new decisions, new obstacles, or new opportunities, we forget to connect it to our pasts. We forget to ask, "Which of these choices best fits with my story so far?"

In the future, you want to be able to tell your whole story honestly and not feel forced to skip or disguise any parts.

The biblical account of Joseph in the Old Testament illustrates these life-story dynamics. Joseph faced dilemmas he could never have expected, and at times he was forced to choose between no-win options. In extremely difficult situations, he made choices in harmony with a consistent pattern in his life of God-centered integrity and faithfulness. Joseph was later fully rewarded for this.

We, too, can look at God's providential care in our lives up to this point, and make choices now that fully align with what God has already done for us.

In contrast with Joseph, his brothers were forced to live a lie for many years because of a tragic choice they made and to see their father's broken heart as a consequence of it.

Every decision you make becomes part of your story. *What is the story you want to tell?* Will it be, "I cast my care upon my heavenly Father, and I obeyed God to the best of my ability"?

Write your story well—and live your story well—because in the future you want to be able to tell the whole story. What you do now really does matter.

VIDEO NOTES

_____

_____

_____

_____

_____

_____

_____

_____

_____

_____

_____

_____

_____

_____

_____

_____

_____

_____

_____

_____

DISCUSSION QUESTIONS

1. Why are the decisions we make so important in shaping the kinds of stories our lives portray?

2. In your own life story up to this point, how would you compare the relative significance of (a) the decisions and choices you've made, and (b) the circumstances and realities of your environment, which you had no say in? Which set of factors had the most influence on you?

3. In your observation, what are some typical poor or unwise decisions that people seem most reluctant to talk about?

4. How easy is it for you to identify with the story of Joseph in the Old Testament? To what degree do you think we *should* be able to relate to his story?

5. What are the most important elements that you want to include in your future story?

6. How do you think your future story will be impacted by the things that have already happened in your past?

MILEPOSTS

- The multitude of experiences and significant moments in any season of our lives will later be condensed into just a few sentences, as we tell our life stories.

- As we make important decisions in the present, it's wise to think about our futures and to ask ourselves, "What story do I want to tell?"

- We want to write our stories well—and live our stories well.

MOVING FORWARD

Again, think about any tough and significant choices you're facing right now or any that you see approaching on the horizon. How will it affect your decision-making process to ask the question: "What story do I want to tell?"

Meanwhile, if you're *not* currently facing such a choice, how can you be better prepared to ask this question when you suddenly encounter a tough and unexpected decision that must be made?

CHANGING YOUR MIND

These words of Joseph from the Old Testament came at a critical

point in his life—reminding us of our need for big-picture, life-story

thinking in our own decision-making moments:

How then could I do such a wicked thing
and sin against God?
Genesis 39:9b

PREPARATION FOR SESSION 3

To help you get ready for Session 3, use these suggested devotions during the week leading up to your small group meeting.

Day One

In the epic life of David as narrated in the Old Testament, we find a potentially explosive incident occurring in 1 Samuel 24. The context is a time of extreme tension in Israel. King Saul has been rejected by God, but still occupies the throne; David, God's choice as the new king, is on the run from Saul, who seeks to kill him.

Read what happens in 1 Samuel 24:1–4. In their hiding place in the cave, what thoughts do you think might have been going through the minds of David and his men at this point? And what do you think you would have done if you were in David's place in that cave?

Day Two

Read what happens next inside the cave in 1 Samuel 24:5–7. What factors do you think triggered David's conscience to move him as it did?

Day Three

Beginning in 1 Samuel 24:8, we see David's confrontation with Saul outside the cave. Read carefully verses 8–11. What principles and influences are guiding and controlling David's actions? And what relationship might these have to your life?

Day Four

Continue reading the rest of David's words to Saul outside the cave in 1 Samuel 24:12–15. How does David demonstrate that he's trusting God and fully placing his life under God's control?

Day Five

In 1 Samuel 24:16–22, notice Saul's response to David and how this incident concludes. (You might also want to check out a similar incident in 1 Samuel 26, as well as explore the remaining episodes in David's conflict with Saul in 1 Samuel 27–31 and 2 Samuel 1–5.) What compelling evidence do you see that God was pleased with how David responded to his conscience that day in the cave?

Last Session

In a significant decision-making time, if we'll ask ourselves, *What story do I want to tell?* we'll be more likely to avoid decisions that later cause regret.

Pay Attention to the Tension

Often we lean toward a certain choice or option, latching onto it emotionally because it seems to offer us one of three things: pleasure, promotion, or profit. So, with our decisions in hand, we're ready to push ahead.

And yet there might be a little something in the back of our minds or hearts that wants to hold us back. There's a little question mark somewhere about whether this decision might involve something that's not entirely right ethically or morally.

What do we with that?

When one of those questions or issues pops up, it's easy to dismiss it by telling ourselves, "Everyone else is doing it," or, "It's not really such a big deal," or, "No one thinks that way anymore," or, "No one will even know." We're quick to squelch the tension we feel.

But there's a better way to respond. Let's find out what it is.

DISCUSSION STARTER

What's your understanding of the purpose of your *conscience?* Why do human beings need a conscience—or *do* they?

VIDEO OVERVIEW

For Session 3 of the DVD

When we face those tough, unwanted decisions, our third question to ask is this:

Is there a tension that needs my attention?

Many times, as we lean toward a specific option or choice, we sense a degree of tension that's rooted in a moral or ethical issue. We might think of it as a "red flag," or "a twinge of conscience." Something doesn't seem exactly right, and this makes us hesitate.

Sometimes we don't sense the tension until someone else makes us aware of the issue involved. Or we might be aware of the tension, yet try to discount or ignore it.

Whenever we face such tension, it's best to pause and allow it to rise up and become as "big" as it can possibly get. Otherwise, if we ignore the tension and plunge ahead into the decision we favor, we might end up at a place we later regret.

We're easily tempted to disregard the tension because we so easily get emotionally attached to a certain option or choice. That emotion acts like adrenaline and adds momentum to the direction we want to go.

That's why we need to force ourselves to pay attention to the tension.

In the Bible, an incident in the life of the young man David illustrates this kind of tension awareness. While a fugitive on the run from King Saul, David was handed a perfect opportunity to kill Saul, but his conscience prevented him from doing so. David refused to let Saul's wrong behavior become an excuse for his own wrong behavior. Instead, David put the matter entirely into God's hands.

"God takes full responsibility for the life wholly devoted to him"— that's something David believed, as evidenced by his actions. He trusted God for the outcomes of his life.

When we fail to do what David did, we risk being left on our own by God. But instead of taking that risk—and especially since we can never really know the future—we need to entrust our lives to the only One who *does* know the future.

VIDEO NOTES

_____

_____

_____

_____

_____

_____

_____

_____

_____

_____

_____

_____

_____

_____

_____

_____

_____

_____

_____

_____

_____

DISCUSSION QUESTIONS

1. What factors and influences in our culture tend to make us want to ignore the warnings we get from our consciences?

2. Do you think there's anything we can do to make our consciences more sensitive in a helpful and healthy way? If so, what? If not, why not?

3. What part do you think the Holy Spirit plays in making Christians aware of potential moral and ethical dangers in their paths?

4. Do you think there's anything Christians can do to make themselves more open and aware of the Holy Spirit's warnings and guidance? If so, what?

5. What are the factors that allow a person to fully trust God with the details of his or her life?

6. What does it mean for a person to actually let God have full responsibility for the outcomes of his or her life? What important differences will that attitude make in how we live day to day?

MILEPOSTS

- As we lean toward a certain choice or option, we often experience a hesitation or tension that's rooted in some ethical or moral issue involved in such a decision.

- Before we finalize our decisions, it's wise to ask ourselves, "Is there a tension that needs my attention?" We let the tension become as big as it can get, so we can fully consider it before making our decisions.

- Asking that question allows us to avoid making decisions that we might later regret.

MOVING FORWARD

Once more, think about those tough and significant choices you might be facing right now in your life or any that you see looming on the horizon. How will it affect your decision-making process to ask the question: "Is there a tension that needs my attention?"

And if you're *not* currently facing such a choice, how can you be better prepared to ask this question when you do suddenly encounter a tough and unexpected decision?

CHANGING YOUR MIND

At a critical point in David's life, he could have exacted revenge upon someone who had mistreated him, but he wisely chose not to. His example reminds us to "pay attention to the tension":

> *Afterward, David was conscience-stricken ...*
> *He said to his men,*
> *"The Lord forbid that I should do such a thing ..."*
> *1 Samuel 24:5–6*

PREPARATION FOR SESSION 4

To help you get ready for Session 4, use these suggested devotions during the week leading up to your small group meeting.

Day One

Jesus talks to his followers in Matthew 5:14–16 about the influence they are to have in the world. What's the "bottom line" of this influence, according to verse 16? And what kind of factors do you think will allow this kind of result to happen?

Day Two

The words that the apostle Paul writes in 1 Corinthians 6:18–20 are in the context of his teaching on sexual purity. Notice the main idea he gives at the end of verse 20. Paul also states reasons we should live this way. What are those reasons, and what do they mean in your life?

Day Three

Paul goes on in 1 Corinthians 10:31 to state an even broader principle. How would you express this instruction in your own words? And is there anything in our lives that this instruction does *not* pertain to?

Day Four

Look at the statement made about God and what he gives us in James 1:17. How does the truth of this statement relate to the accomplishments and successes that we achieve in life?

Day Five

Notice the picture Jesus gives us in John 15:5 and especially the concluding statement he gives at the end of this verse. How would you say this picture relates to the accomplishments and successes that we achieve in life?

Last Session

In a significant decision-making time, if we'll ask ourselves, *Is there a tension that needs my attention?* we will be more likely to escape the kind of moral and ethical dangers that can eventually jeopardize our futures.

SESSION 4

Passing It On

The three questions we've looked at so far are the kind that most people can see the value of. You don't even have to believe in God to appreciate them and to apply them.

But our fourth question is different. It's especially for those who believe that God is personal, that he knows our names, that he even has a plan and purpose for everyone's life. And it's especially for those who believe that Jesus is the Son of God who died for our sins and who rose from the dead to elevate our lives into an entirely new dimension.

This final question points the way to moving our lives upward into that new dimension. It's about seeing our lives in a far broader context; it's about looking ahead and seeing a wider, bolder, and more beautiful horizon. It's about connecting with something so much bigger and higher than anything we've experienced in life so far.

It's something we all deeply long for—because it's rooted in the image of God that's imprinted on all human beings.

DISCUSSION STARTER

Think of the people you know that have the most significant accomplishments in their lives. How much do they say about their accomplishments, and what seems to be their attitude about all that they have achieved?

VIDEO OVERVIEW

For Session 4 of the DVD

Whenever we're praised for something, Christians believe that we're not to hang on to that glory. Instead, God created us to say thank you, and then look for a way to pass along or transfer that glory to him.

We all know people who are glory hounds. By hoarding whatever credit or honor or recognition they receive, they end up becoming smaller in the esteem of others, not greater. We actually come to think more highly of someone who does not hoard the glory for his or her accomplishments than we do of someone who does.

Although we were created to do amazing things, we weren't created to cling to the glory that comes from those things. If we do, the glory of those accomplishments grows smaller, not greater.

The glory for these things belongs properly to God because all our talents and abilities and opportunities are ultimately from him. Apart from him, we could do nothing of significance. It's God who sets us up for success. So the honor and glory for anything good we do belongs to our heavenly Father.

So here's the fourth question to ask whenever we face tough, unwanted decisions: *What would be most honoring to God?*

This theme of the glory that belongs to God is found throughout the Bible. We see it when the apostle Paul reminds us that because our bodies are temples of the Holy Spirit, *"Therefore honor God with your body"* (1 Corinthians 6:20b). We see it also in the words Jesus gave his followers: *"Let your light shine before men, that they might see your good deeds and praise your Father in heaven"* (Matthew 5:16).

What would be most honoring to God? That's a dangerous question, one that leads us beyond mere issues of right and wrong. Answering it honestly brings radical changes in our lives, because everybody lives for *somebody's* glory, but living for our own glory ultimately makes us insignificant. Living for God's glory, on the other hand, leads to our freedom and to a life that others celebrate.

VIDEO NOTES

_____

_____

_____

_____

_____

_____

_____

_____

_____

_____

_____

_____

_____

_____

_____

_____

DISCUSSION QUESTIONS

1. In general, as you observe people, what evidence do you see that we all desire to achieve significant accomplishments and to be connected with something bigger than ourselves?

2. How would you define the word *glory*—in terms that just about anyone would understand?

3. Why is "hoarding" glory so detrimental to a person and so unattractive to others who see it in that person?

4. Why is it appropriate for God to receive glory for all our true
    accomplishments? What does this say about who God is
    and what he's like?

5. How can we become more aware of how to give greater
    glory to God?

6. What do you want your funeral to be like? What would you
    like others to say about you? How do you want them to feel
    about you?

MILEPOSTS

- All of us live for *somebody's* glory. But those who live for their own glory ultimately lose that glory and instead become small and insignificant.

- We were all created to do remarkable things and to transfer the glory for those things to God—since he alone makes them possible.

- In our moments of decision, as we consider various choices and options, it's always wise to ask ourselves, "What would be most honoring to God?"

MOVING FORWARD

Think about the choices you'll be making in the immediate future. There might be much at stake or maybe not so much (as far as you can foresee), but they're the most important decisions you face right now. Whether they are big or little decisions, how will it affect your decision-making process to ask the question: "What would be most honoring to God?"

CHANGING YOUR MIND

These New Testament words remind us to always keep God's glory at

the forefront of our minds and motives:

. . . let your light shine before men,
that they may see your good deeds
and praise your Father in heaven.
Matthew 5:16

. . . you were bought at a price.
Therefore honor God with your body.
1 Corinthians 6:20

Leader's Guide

So, You're the Leader...

Is that intimidating? Perhaps exciting? No doubt you have some mental pictures of what it will look like, what you will say, and how it will go. Before you get too far into the planning process, there are some things you should know about leading a small group discussion. We've compiled some tried and true techniques here to help you.

Basics About Leading

1. Cultivate discussion — It's also easy to think that the meeting lives or dies by your ideas. In reality, what makes a small group meeting successful are the ideas of everyone in the group. The most valuable thing you can do is to get people to share their thoughts. That's how the relationships in your group will grow and thrive. Here's a rule: The impact of your study material will typically never exceed the impact of the relationships through which it was studied. The more meaningful the relationships, the more meaningful the study. In a sterile environment, even the best material is suppressed.

2. Point to the material — A good host or hostess gets the party going by offering delectable hors d'oeuvres and beverages. You too should be ready to serve up "delicacies" from the material. Sometimes you will simply read the discussion questions and invite everyone to respond. At other times, you may encourage others to share their ideas. Remember, some of the best treats are the ones your guests will bring to the party. Go with the flow of the meeting, and be ready to pop out of the kitchen as needed.

3. Depart from the material — We have carefully designed this study for your small group. But that doesn't mean you should follow every part word for word. Knowing how and when to depart from the material is a valuable art. Nobody knows more about your people than you do. The narratives, questions, and exercises are here to provide a framework for discovery. However, every group is motivated differently. Sometimes the best way to start a small group discussion is simply to ask, "Does anyone have a personal insight or revelation you'd like to share from this week's material?" Then sit back and listen.

4. Stay on track — Although this may seem contradictory to the previous point, there is an art to facilitating an engaging conversation. While you want to leave some space for your group members to process the discussion, you need to keep your objectives in mind. If your goal is to have a meaningful experience with this material, then you should make sure the discussion is contributing to that end. It's easy to get off on a tangent. Be prepared to interject politely and refocus the group. You may need to say something like, "Excuse me, we're obviously all interested in this subject; however, I just want to make sure we cover all the material for this week."

5. Above all, pray — The best communicators are the ones that manage to get out of God's way enough to let him communicate *through* them. That's important to keep in mind. Books don't teach God's Word; neither do sermons nor group discussions. God himself speaks into the hearts of men and women, and prayer is our vital channel to communicate directly with him. Cover your efforts in prayer. You don't just want God present at your meeting; you want him to direct it.

We hope you find these suggestions helpful. And we hope you enjoy leading this study. You will find additional guidelines and suggestions for each session in the Leader's Guide notes that follow.

Leader's Guide
Session Notes

Session 1 — Really

Bottom Line

All of us face difficult decisions that have potentially life-changing impacts. But even when facing such critical choices, we tend to get emotionally connected to a particular option or direction without being fully honest with ourselves. To make the best choices, we need to push toward greater self-honesty.

Discussion Starter

Use the "Discussion Starter" printed in Session 1 of the Participant's Guide to "break the ice"—and to help everyone see that self- deception is a tendency we all have to battle against.

Video Overview

The Video Overview section for Session 1 will help group members identify certain themes or questions before they watch the DVD clip. As leader, you may choose to read or summarize this section for the group, or have a volunteer read it.

If you haven't done so already, at this point insert the DVD and choose

Session 1 from the Group Curriculum menu options.

Notes for Discussion Questions

1. **If you're willing to share this with the group, what are some**

    of the most unexpected and uncomfortable decisions you've

    had to make in your life? In contrast, of all your life's most

    significant decisions, which were the *easiest* **to make?**

    Share your own response, which will be the best encourage-

    ment for thorough, honest answers from the rest of the group.

2. **What choices in your life are you most grateful for? And how**

    close did you come to making an entirely different decision?

    Again, your own genuine response will help open up everyone

    else in the group to share candidly.

3. **In your observation, what are some of the reasons people of-**

    ten seem reluctant to be fully honest with themselves about

    the reasons for the choices they make?

    Help direct the discussion to the reasons given in the DVD

    teaching content, but also welcome other observations from

    the group members.

4. **When it's time to make a major decision, what helps you to be more honest with yourself as you consider your true motives and desires?**

Most of us need lots of help in becoming more honest with ourselves, so allow plenty of time for discussion here.

5. **Do you know people who seem more committed to seeking truth than they are to seeking their own happiness?**

The goal here is to help the group recognize that truth seekers are rarer than happiness seekers. In fact, we *all* seek our own happiness to a significant extent, and much of that longing is actually rooted in how God made us and what he designed us to long for (finding our true *joy* in him). Ultimately, this desire for joy, in its pure form, is itself fully linked with God's truth—so by genuinely seeking one, we seek both.

6. **What most convinces you that the human heart is inclined toward self-deception?**

The most foundational answer is that this fact is stated to us authoritatively in the Bible, God's revealed truth—as seen in Jeremiah 17:9 as well as in other passages.

Moving Forward

The goal here is to help group members build the habit into their lives of regularly asking, "Am I being completely honest with myself?"

Preparation for Session 2

Remember to point out the brief daily devotions that the group members can complete and which will help greatly in stimulating discussion in your next session. These devotions will enable everyone to dig into the Bible and start wrestling with the topics that will come up next time.

Session 2 — The Story of Your Life

Bottom Line

When we face tough decisions, we'll make the wisest choices when we make them in light of the big picture—our life stories as already begun and developed in our pasts, as well as the continuing stories we want to see in our futures. We want to live our stories well—and be able to tell them unashamedly.

Discussion Starter

Use the "Discussion Starter" listed for Session 2 of the Participant's Guide. This one should help everyone in your group focus on the potential power and influence of our life stories—and how these stories tend to compress lots of experiences into a minimum of words.

Video Overview

The Video Overview section for Session 2 will help group members identify certain themes or questions before they watch the DVD clip. As leader, you may choose to read or summarize this section for the group, or have a volunteer read it.

If you haven't done so already, at this point insert the DVD and choose Session 2 from the Group Curriculum menu options.

Notes for Discussion Questions

1. **Why are the decisions we make so important in shaping the kinds of stories our lives portray?**

    This question can help reinforce for your group the fact that life truly is a progressive sequence of the decisions we make.

2. **In your own life story up to this point, how would you compare the relative significance of (a) the decisions and choices you've made, and (b) the circumstances and realities of your environment, which you had no say in? Which set of factors had the most influence on you?**

    Some in your group might point out this interesting fact: many times, even circumstances and environmental realities that we have no control over will impact our lives only to the extent that we *let* them. This is especially true as we grow older. Even here, our own choices have great power.

3. **In your observation, what are some typical poor or unwise decisions that people seem most reluctant to talk about?**

    This will help your group see clearly the common reality of elements in our life stories that we regret and wish we could change. This might be a great opportunity to bring in the good news of our redemption and new life in Christ, all made pos-sible by his death as the punishment for our sins and his rising from the dead to guarantee our own new existence. He allows us a fresh start in life that's fueled every day by his forgiveness for our sinful mistakes of the past.

4. **How easy is it for you to identify with the story of Joseph in the Old Testament? To what degree do you think we *should* be able to relate to his story?**

It might be difficult at first for everyone to identify with some-one as remote from us as Joseph—and someone of such stel-lar character. But we can all embrace his example of learning to see God's sovereign hand at work in all the obstacles we face in life and to see the value of choosing to stay faithful to God and his standards even when such decisions are costly.

5. **What are the most important elements that you want to in-clude in your future story?**

Let your honest answer lead the way for others. Think espe-cially of what you most want God to accomplish in your life.

6.   **How do you think your future story will be impacted by the things that have already happened in your past?**

Again, this could be an opportune moment for bringing in the power of the gospel—power to not only redeem us from our pasts, but also to transform the perceived "negatives" in our backgrounds to open doors of gospel ministry to others who struggle with similar situations.

Moving Forward

The goal here is to help group members build the habit into their lives of regularly asking, "What story do I want to tell?"

Preparation for Session 3

Again, encourage your group members to complete the brief daily devotions. These will help stimulate discussion in your next session. They'll enable everyone to dig into the Bible and start wrestling with the topics coming up next time.

Session 3 — Pay Attention to the Tension

Bottom Line

God has designed us so that we can be adequately warned by our consciences or by the Holy Spirit whenever potential moral and ethical dangers lie in our paths. That's why we do well to "pay attention to the tension" whenever we face significant decisions, so we can avoid choices that we would later regret.

Discussion Starter

Again, use the "Discussion Starter" listed for Session 3 of the Participant's Guide. This should help the group grasp our need for some kind of "warning system" to alert us about potential ethical and moral hazards on our horizon.

Video Overview

The Video Overview section for Session 3 will help group members identify certain themes or questions before they watch the DVD clip. As leader, you may choose to read or summarize this section for the group, or have a volunteer read it.

If you haven't done so already, at this point insert the DVD and choose Session 3 from the Group Curriculum menu options.

Notes for Discussion Questions

1. **What factors and influences in our culture tend to make us want to ignore the warnings we get from our consciences?**

    This should help the group recognize that the importance of listening to our consciences and to the Holy Spirit is seldom reinforced by our culture. More commonly, it's actively opposed or belittled.

2. **Do you think there's anything we can do to make our consciences more sensitive, in a helpful and healthy way? If so, what? If not, why not?**

    You might want to call attention to passages such as Acts 24:16 (where Paul gives us the example of "striving" to keep his conscience clear); 1 Timothy 1:5 (which links a "good conscience" with purity of heart and sincerity of faith); 1 Timothy 4:2 (which highlights how habitual lying can leave a conscience "seared"); Hebrews 10:19–22 (which encourages our appropriation of the cleansing power of Jesus' blood upon our consciences); and 1 Peter 3:21 (which affirms baptism "as an appeal to God for a good conscience").

3. **What part do you think the Holy Spirit plays in making Christians aware of potential moral and ethical dangers in their paths?**

    Help your group understand that the Holy Spirit often works

through our consciences, but is also distinct from our consciences and always a higher authority than our consciences.
You might want to look at promises about the Holy Spirit, such
as the ones Jesus gave to his followers in John 16:13 *("When
he, the Spirit of truth, comes, he will guide you into all truth")* and
John 14:26 *("The Counselor, the Holy Spirit, whom the Father will
send in my name, will teach you all things and will remind you of
everything I have said to you")*.

4. **Do you think there's anything Christians can do to make
    themselves more open and aware of the Holy Spirit's warn-
    ings and guidance? If so, what?**

    Because of our human sinfulness, our consciences are fallible;
    the Holy Spirit, however, is *infallible*, and his ministry to us is
    always perfectly conformed to God's will (Romans 8:27). You
    might want to call attention to passages that steer us away
    from "grieving" the Holy Spirit (Ephesians 4:30–31), "resisting"
    the Spirit (Acts 7:51), or "quenching" the Spirit's fire (1 Thessa-
    lonians 5:19–22).

5.   **What are the factors that allow a person to fully trust God with the details of his or her life?**

Some of the factors that might arise in your discussion include a sufficient awareness of God's love and trustworthiness and especially an appreciation of his personal care for us and his commitment to each of us. The giving over to death of his Son Jesus is the everlasting proof of God's love for us, showing beyond all possible doubt that he is worthy to be entrusted with our lives.

6.   **What does it mean for a person to actually let God have full responsibility for the outcomes of his or her life? What important differences will that attitude make in how we live day to day?**

Perhaps the greatest benefit that might be mentioned here is the sense of peace we can enjoy when we fully trust God for all our tomorrows.

Moving Forward

The value here is in helping the group members learn to consciously stop and carefully evaluate their spiritual and emotional heart conditions whenever a "bump" situation occurs. Remind them of how valuable this habit will become.

Preparation for Session 4

Again, encourage your group members to complete the daily devotions. This will help them be better prepared for the topics coming up next time.

Session 4 — Passing It On

Bottom Line

We all live for *someone's* glory—but living for our own glory will ul-timately trap us in insignificance. God has created us to deflect to him the glory for all our accomplishments—which is only right, since he alone makes these achievements possible. Living for God's glory opens up our lives to unprecedented freedom and fulfillment.

Discussion Starter

Again, use the "Discussion Starter" listed for Session 4 of the Partici-pant's Guide. This should help everyone in the group see that "glory hounds" always defeat their own self-seeking purposes, while those who do *not* live for their own glory end up being more appreciated and praised than those who do.

Video Overview

The Video Overview section for Session 4 will help group members identify certain themes or questions before they watch the DVD clip. As leader, you may choose to read or summarize this section for the group, or have a volunteer read it.

If you haven't done so already, at this point insert the DVD and choose Session 4 from the Group Curriculum menu options.

Notes for Discussion Questions

1. **In general, as you observe people, what evidence do you see that we all desire to achieve significant accomplishments and to be connected with something bigger than ourselves?**
    You might want to mention the ways in which you've personally sensed this desire throughout your own life.

2. **How would you define the word *glory*—in terms that just about anyone would understand?**
    This word *glory* can be connected to concepts of fame, praise, honor, gratitude, weighty significance, and more.

3. **Why is "hoarding" glory so detrimental to a person and so unattractive to others who see it in that person?**
    This question could spark some interesting discussion. We all seem to dislike a "glory hound"—but why, exactly?

4.   **Why is it appropriate for God to receive glory for all our true accomplishments? What does this say about who God is and what he's like?**

Allow adequate time to articulate praise and thanksgiving for God's infinite goodness, mercy, wisdom, power, and other attributes. God is pleased—and we are strengthened and enriched—when we make ourselves more consciously aware of these things.

5.   **How can we become more aware of how to give greater glory to God?**

Especially helpful here is learning to recognize more of what God is actively doing in everything we're involved with. Also, greater recognition of our own weaknesses and failures can help us see more clearly how dependent we are on God to accomplish anything.

6.   **What do you want your funeral to be like? What would you like others to say about you? How do you want them to feel about you?**

Share your honest response here, encouraging everyone to do the same. As you close, ask each person in the group to pray a sentence prayer that gives glory to God for who he is and for what he does in our lives.

Moving Forward

The goal here is to help the group members build the habit into their

lives of regularly asking, "What would be most honoring to God?"

Staying in Love

Falling in Love Is Easy, Staying in Love Requires a Plan

Andy Stanley

We all know what's required to fall in love...a pulse. Falling in love is easy. But staying there— that's something else entirely. With more than a thousand matchmaking services available today and new ones springing up all the time, finding a romantic match can be easier than ever. But staying together with the one you've found seems to be the real challenge.

So, is it possible for two people to fall in love and actually stay there? Absolutely! Let pastor and author Andy Stanley show you how in this four-session, video-based study that also features a separate participant's guide.

Session titles include:
1. The Juno Dilemma
2. Re-Modeling
3. Feelin' It
4. Multiple Choice Marriage

Available in stores and online!

Faith, Hope, and Luck

Discover What You Can Expect from God

Andy Stanley

Our faith in God often hinges on his activity—or inactivity—in our daily experiences. When our prayers are answered, our faith soars. When God is silent, it becomes harder to trust him. When God shows up in an unmistakable way, our confidence in him reaches new heights. But when he doesn't come through, our confidence often wanes.

But it doesn't have to be that way—it's not supposed to be that way.

This five-session study is guaranteed to transform your thinking about faith. As you listen or watch, you will discover the difference between faith and hope. You will be presented with a definition of faith that will shed new light on both the Old and New Testaments. Andy Stanley explains what we can expect of God every time we come to him with a request. In addition, he exposes the flaws in what some have labeled The Faith Movement.

With both a DVD and separate participant's guide, *Faith, Hope, and Luck* is not just another group study. This content is foundational for everyone who desires to be an informed, active follower of Christ.

Five sessions include:

1. Better Odds
2. Betting on Hope
3. Beating the Odds
4. No Dice
5. All In

Available in stores and online!

Five Things God Uses to Grow Your Faith

Andy Stanley

Imagine how different your outlook on life would be if you had absolute confidence that God was with you. Imagine how differently you would respond to difficulties, temptations, and even good things if you knew with certainty that God was in all of it and was planning to leverage it for good. In other words, imagine what it would be like to have PERFECT faith. In this DVD study, Andy Stanley builds a biblical case for five things God uses to grow BIG faith.

In six video sessions, Andy covers the following topics:
• Big Faith
• Practical Teaching
• Providential Relationships
• Private Disciplines
• Personal Ministry
• Pivotal Circumstances

Along with the separate participant's guide, this resource will equip groups to become more mature followers of Jesus Christ.

Available in stores and online!

Twisting the Truth

Learning to Discern in a
Culture of Deception

Andy Stanley

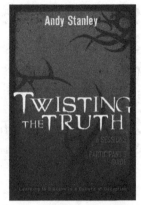

In six insight-packed sessions, Andy Stanley exposes four destructive and all-too-prevalent lies about authority, pain, sex, and sin. They're deceptions powerful enough to ruin our relationships, our lives, even our eternities—but only if we let them. Including both a small group DVD and participant's guide that work together, *Twisting the Truth* untwists the lies that can drag us down. With his gift for straight, to-the-heart communication, Andy Stanley helps us exchange falsehoods for truths that can turn our lives completely around.

Available in stores and online!

Starting Point
Starter Kit

Find Your Place
in the Story

Andy Stanley and the
Starting Point Team

Starting Point is an exploration of God's grand story and where you fit into the narrative.This proven, small group experience is carefully designed to meet the needs of

- Seekers that are curious about Christianity
- Starters that are new to a relationship with Jesus
- Returners that have been away from church for a while

Starting Point is an accepting, conversational environment where people learn about God's story and their places in it. Starting Point helps participants explore the Bible and begin to understand key truths of the Christian faith.

Carefully refined to enhance community, the ten interactive sessions in Starting Point encourage honest exploration. The *Conversation Guide*, which includes a five-disk audio series featuring Andy Stanley, helps each participant enjoy and engage fully with the small group experience.

About This Starter Kit

The *Starting Point Starter Kit* is geared for ministry leaders. It consists of the following:

- Four-color *Starting Point Conversation Guide* containing five audio disks, with over five hours of teaching by Andy Stanley
- *Starter Guide* providing step-by-step instructions on how to successfully launch and sustain the Starting Point ministry
- A Starting Point TNIV Bible
- One-hour leader training DVD
- Interactive CD containing promotional videos, pre-service marketing graphics, leader training tools, and administrative resources

Available in stores and online!

Making Vision Stick

Andy Stanley

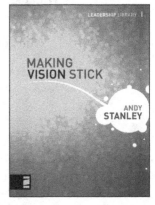

A vision. You as a leader may have it, but has your organization caught it? If a leader's vision is all about what could be and what should be, why are you buried under what is?

Noted author and pastor Andy Stanley points out that if followers don't get the vision, it's because the leaders haven't delivered it. He reveals the three reasons vision doesn't stick. And then he delivers three ways to make vision stick, to make you a leader worth following:

1. Cast vision strategically: defining your vision.
2. Celebrate vision systematically: regularly rejoicing in the successes
3. Live your vision continuously: putting your vision into practice in your own life

With *Making Vision Stick*, you'll learn how to propel you and your organization forward on the vision God has granted you.

Available in stores and online!

Share Your Thoughts

With the Author: Your comments will be forwarded to the author when you send them to *zauthor@zondervan.com*.

With Zondervan: Submit your review of this book by writing to *zreview@zondervan.com*.

Free Online Resources at
www.zondervan.com

Zondervan AuthorTracker: Be notified whenever your favorite authors publish new books, go on tour, or post an update about what's happening in their lives at www.zondervan.com/authortracker.

Daily Bible Verses and Devotions: Enrich your life with daily Bible verses or devotions that help you start every morning focused on God. Visit www.zondervan.com/newsletters.

Free Email Publications: Sign up for newsletters on Christian living, academic resources, church ministry, fiction, children's resources, and more. Visit www.zondervan.com/newsletters.

Zondervan Bible Search: Find and compare Bible passages in a variety of translations at www.zondervanbiblesearch.com.

Other Benefits: Register yourself to receive online benefits like coupons and special offers, or to participate in research.

ZONDERVAN.com/
AUTHORTRACKER
follow your favorite authors